T.E.M.P.

Temporary Emotional
Management Program

De-escalation curriculum

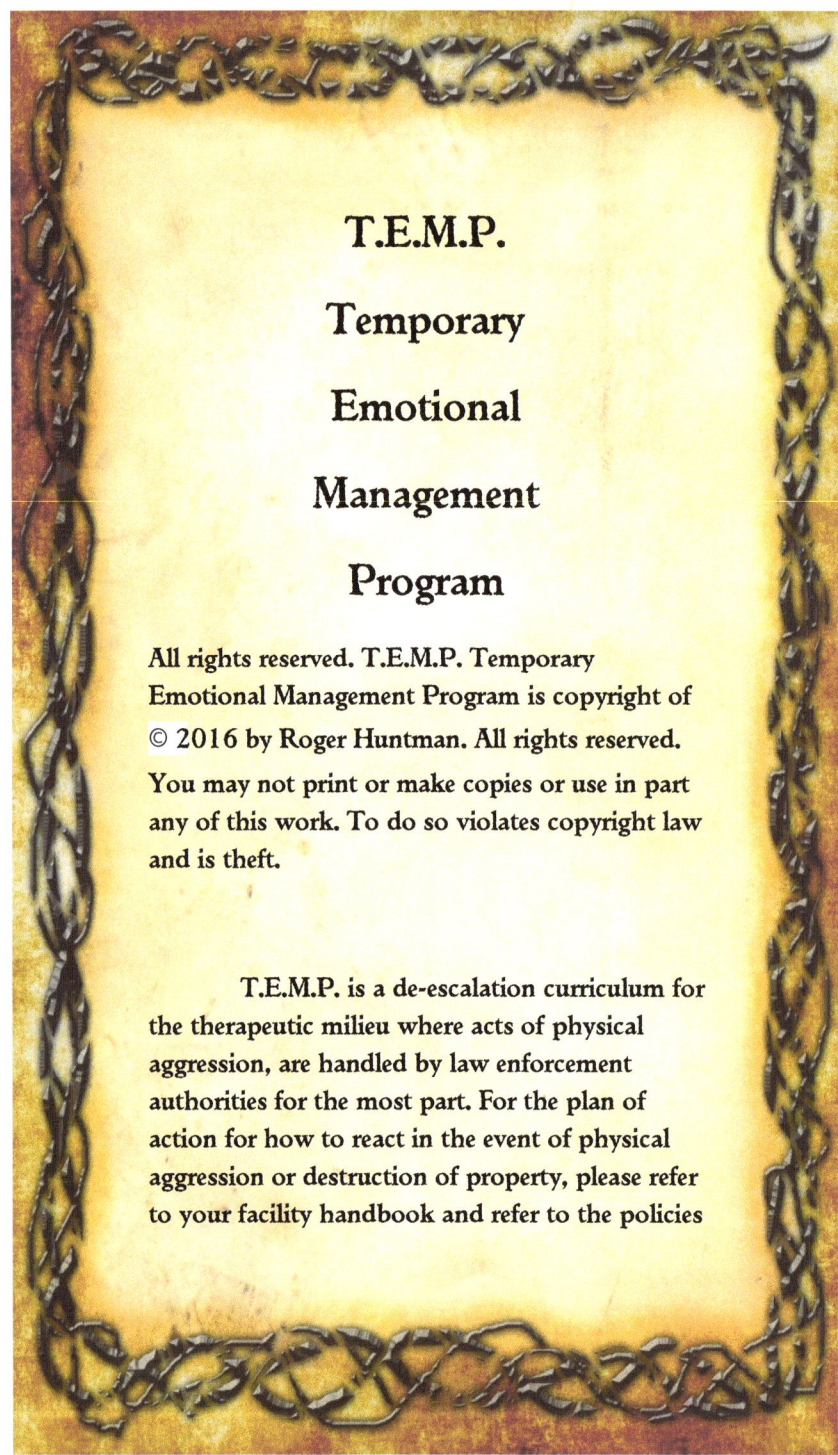

T.E.M.P.

Temporary

Emotional

Management

Program

      T.E.M.P. is a de-escalation curriculum for the therapeutic milieu where acts of physical aggression, are handled by law enforcement authorities for the most part. For the plan of action for how to react in the event of physical aggression or destruction of property, please refer to your facility handbook and refer to the policies

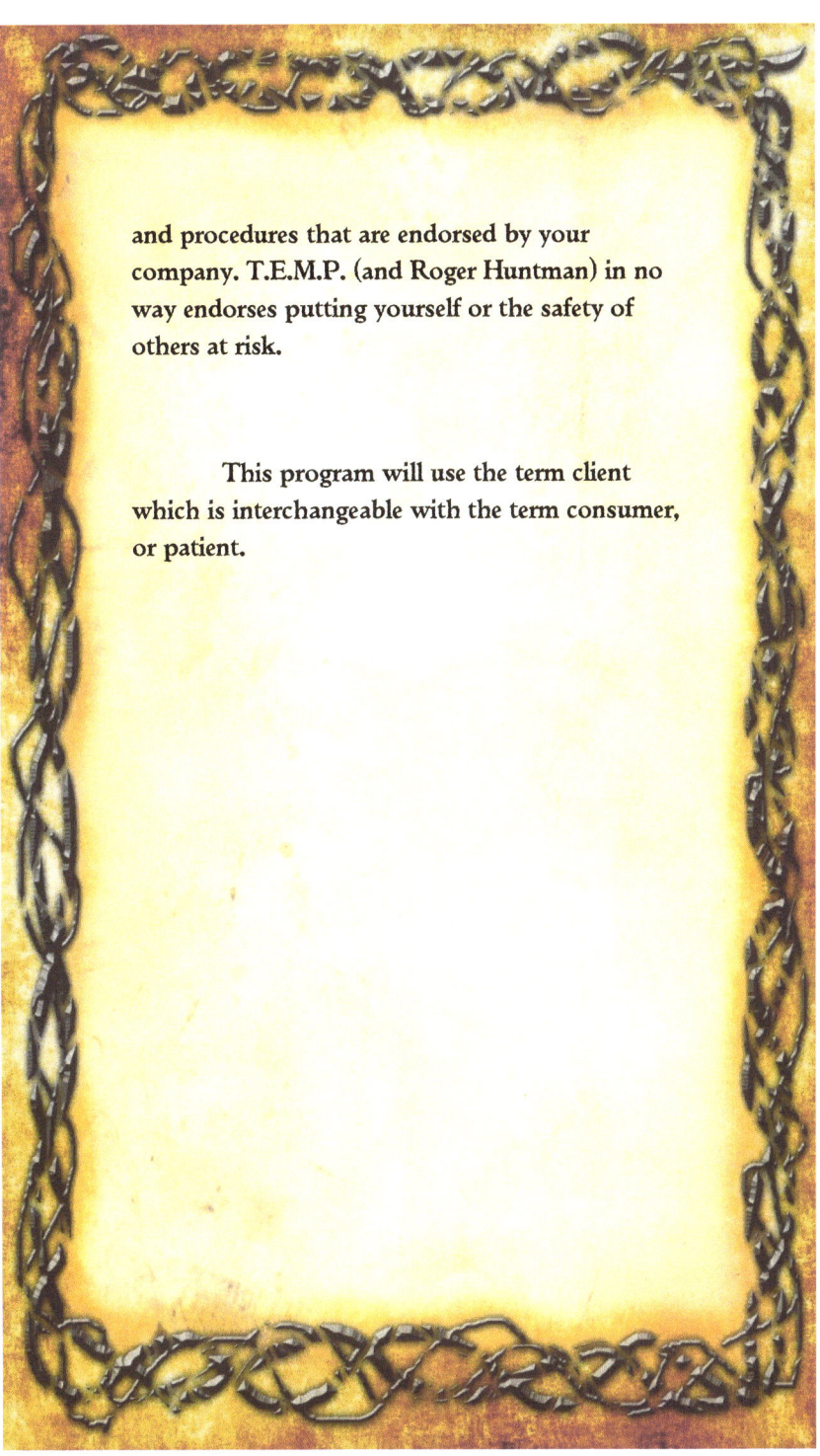

and procedures that are endorsed by your company. T.E.M.P. (and Roger Huntman) in no way endorses putting yourself or the safety of others at risk.

This program will use the term client which is interchangeable with the term consumer, or patient.

Emotions

In almost every type of treatment, the client can be overcome by emotions that affect the decision making abilities. <u>Fear, anger, sadness, and happiness</u> are the most prevalent.

In therapeutic environments there often is a need to temporarily assist a client in regaining emotional peace, as well as bring them back to a state where they can utilize more logic in their decision making skills. This de-escalation is a temporary patch and not a substitute for counselling or therapy. This curriculum is written to assist in communication between the clients and their staff that care for them. In communication between humans, body language can often communicate clues to the mental state that their words cannot.

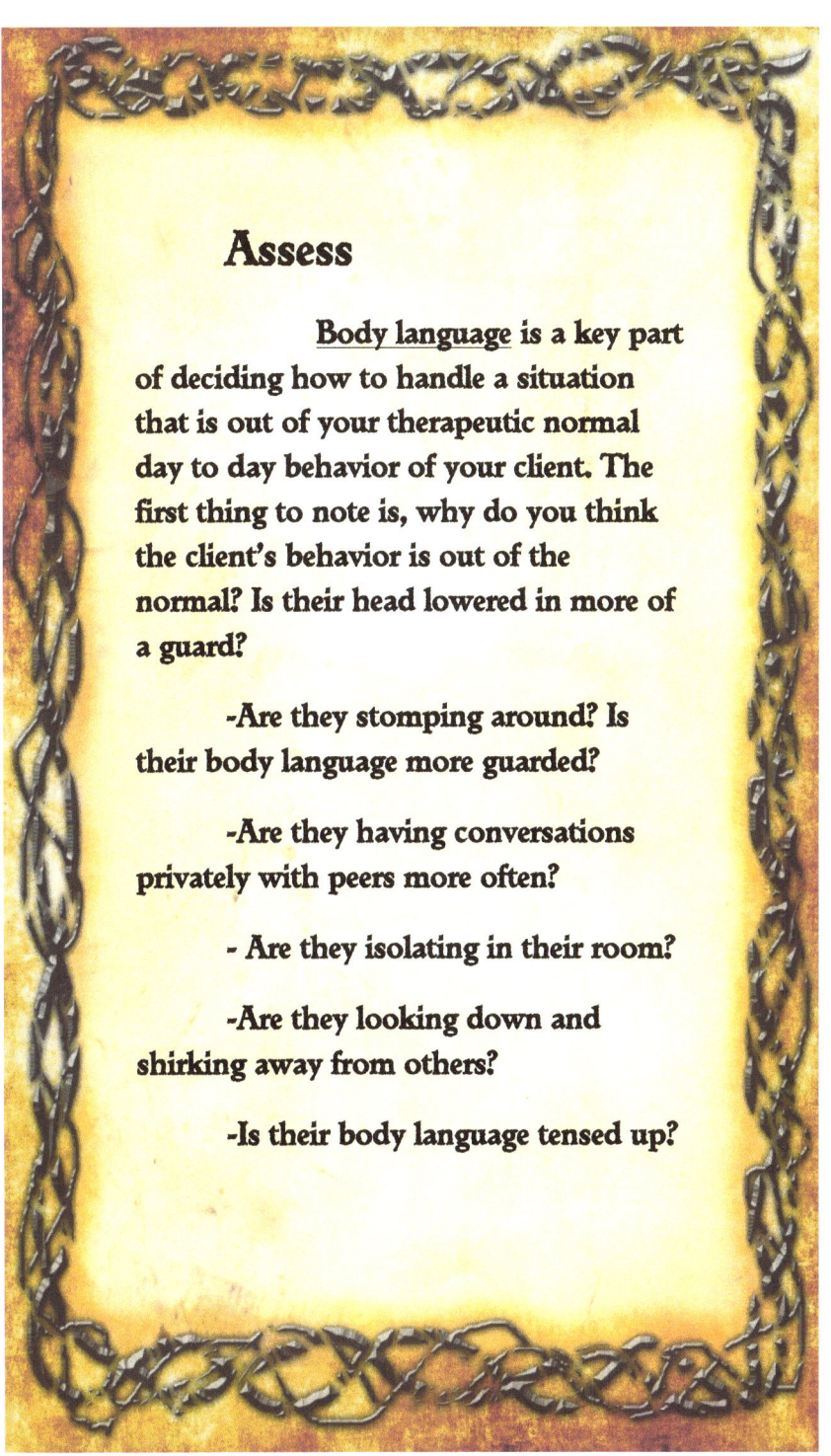

Assess

Body language is a key part of deciding how to handle a situation that is out of your therapeutic normal day to day behavior of your client. The first thing to note is, why do you think the client's behavior is out of the normal? Is their head lowered in more of a guard?

-Are they stomping around? Is their body language more guarded?

-Are they having conversations privately with peers more often?

- Are they isolating in their room?

-Are they looking down and shirking away from others?

-Is their body language tensed up?

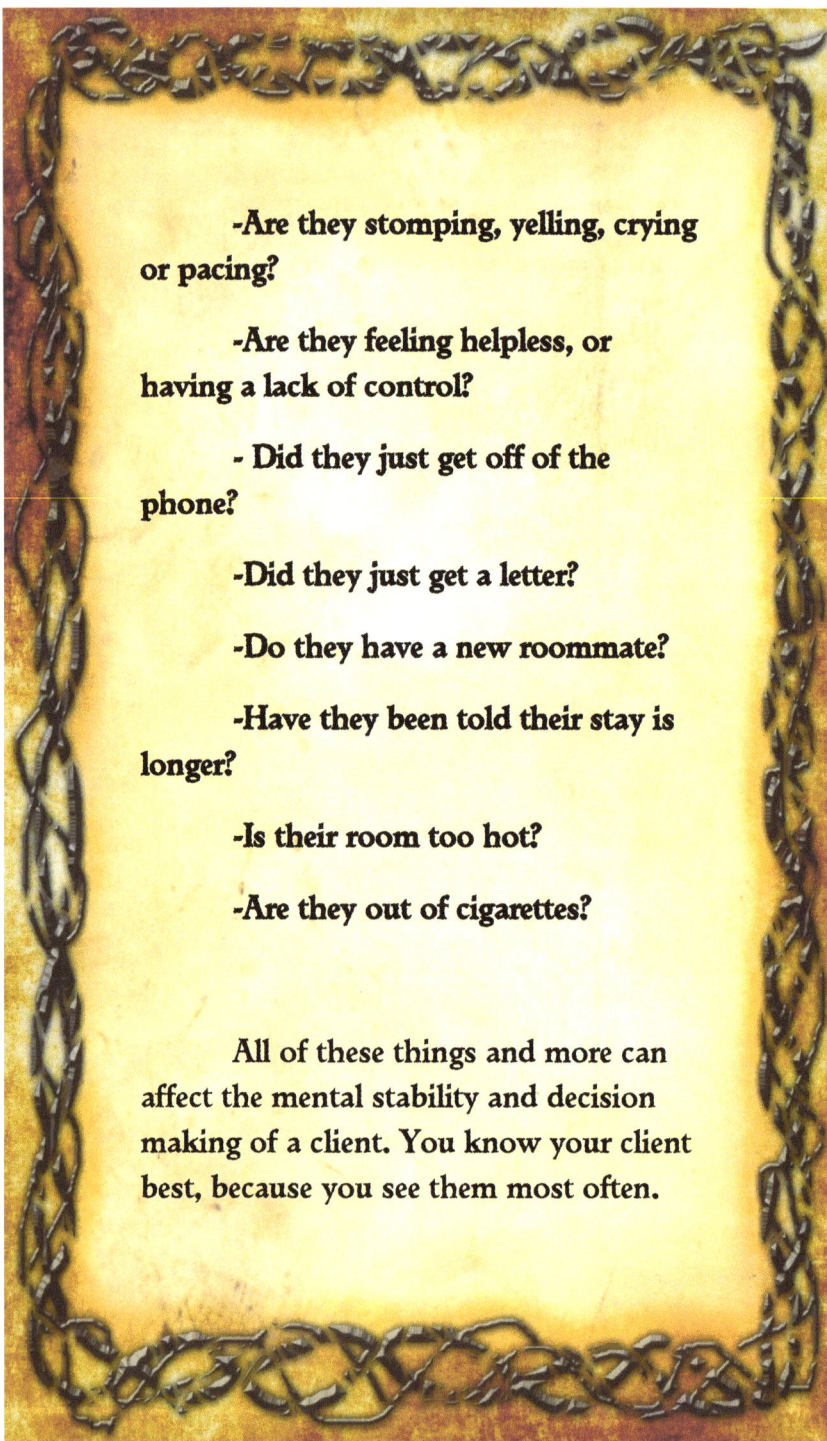

-Are they stomping, yelling, crying or pacing?

-Are they feeling helpless, or having a lack of control?

- Did they just get off of the phone?

-Did they just get a letter?

-Do they have a new roommate?

-Have they been told their stay is longer?

-Is their room too hot?

-Are they out of cigarettes?

All of these things and more can affect the mental stability and decision making of a client. You know your client best, because you see them most often.

You will know what body language is not their norm.

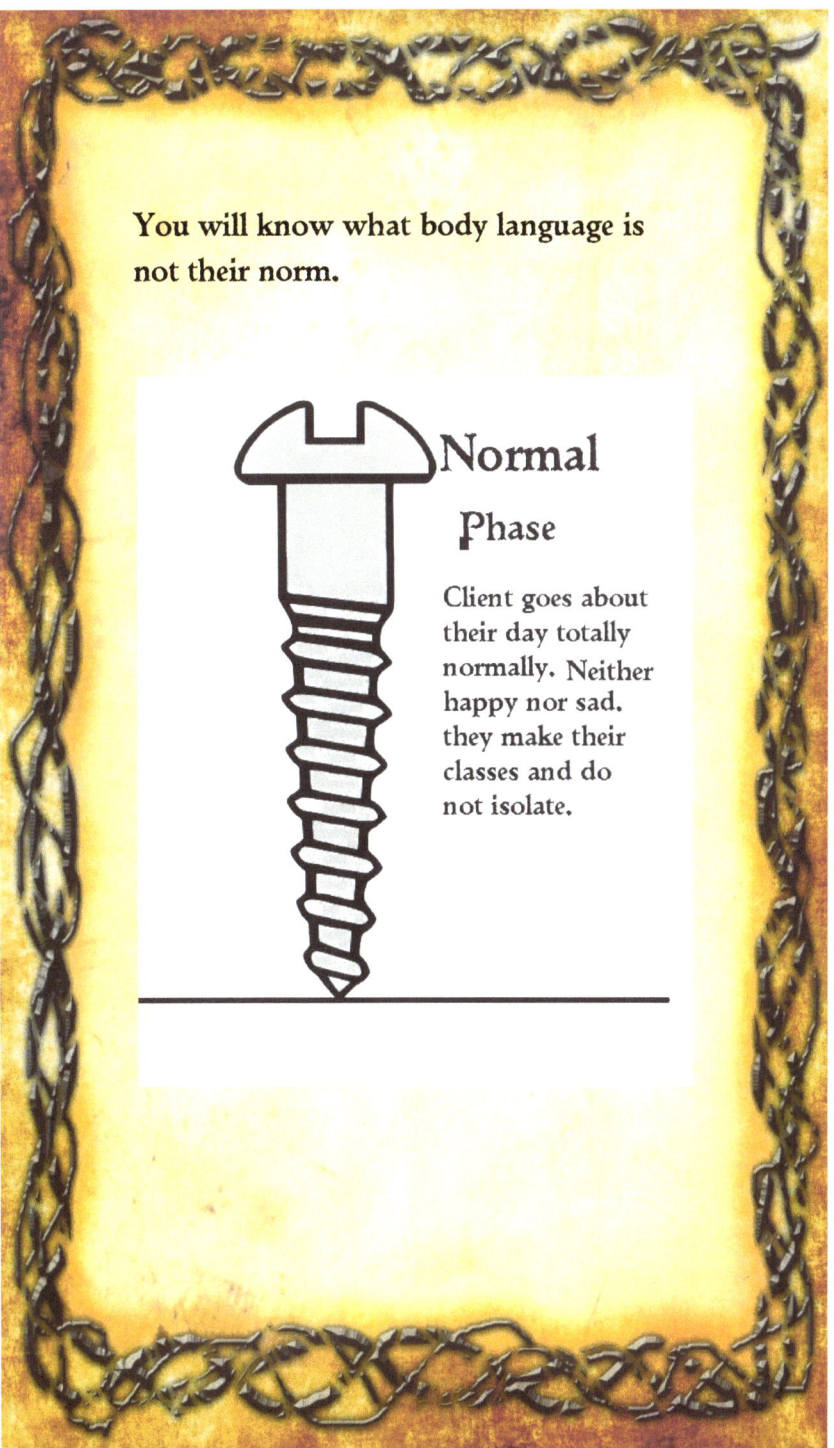

Normal

Phase

Client goes about their day totally normally. Neither happy nor sad. they make their classes and do not isolate.

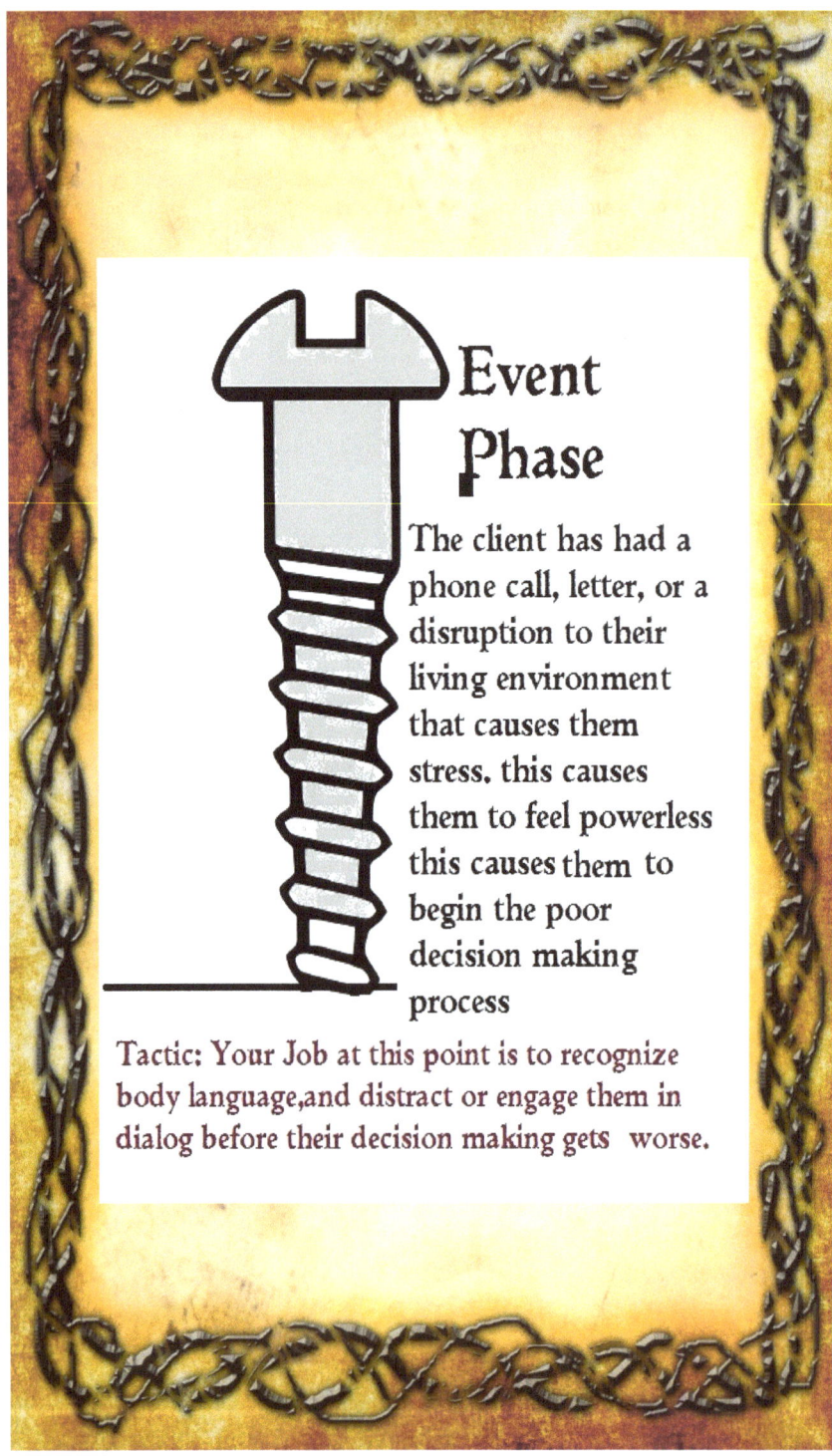

Event Phase

The client has had a phone call, letter, or a disruption to their living environment that causes them stress. this causes them to feel powerless this causes them to begin the poor decision making process

Tactic: Your Job at this point is to recognize body language,and distract or engage them in dialog before their decision making gets worse.

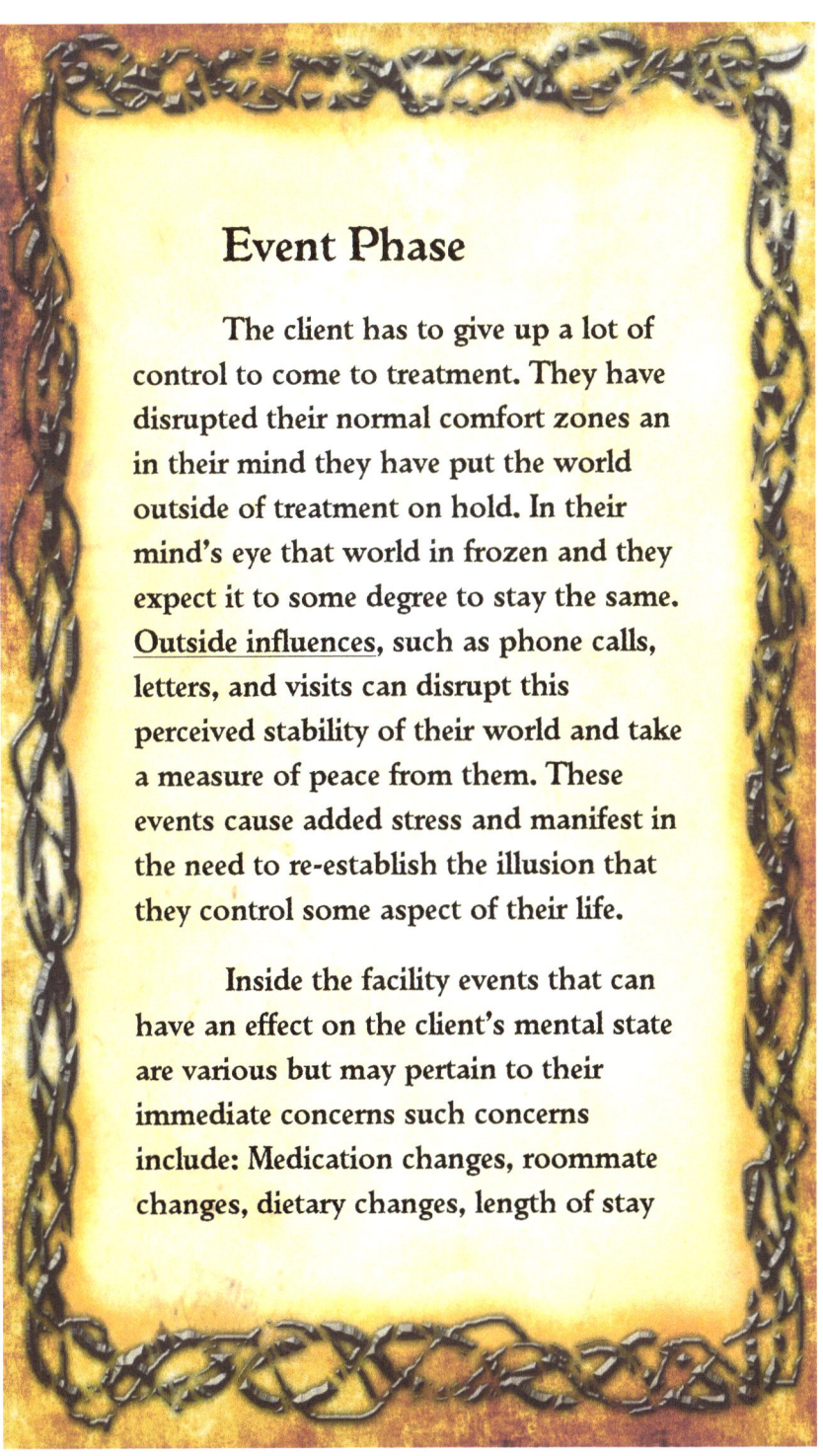

Event Phase

The client has to give up a lot of control to come to treatment. They have disrupted their normal comfort zones an in their mind they have put the world outside of treatment on hold. In their mind's eye that world in frozen and they expect it to some degree to stay the same. <u>Outside influences</u>, such as phone calls, letters, and visits can disrupt this perceived stability of their world and take a measure of peace from them. These events cause added stress and manifest in the need to re-establish the illusion that they control some aspect of their life.

Inside the facility events that can have an effect on the client's mental state are various but may pertain to their immediate concerns such concerns include: Medication changes, roommate changes, dietary changes, length of stay

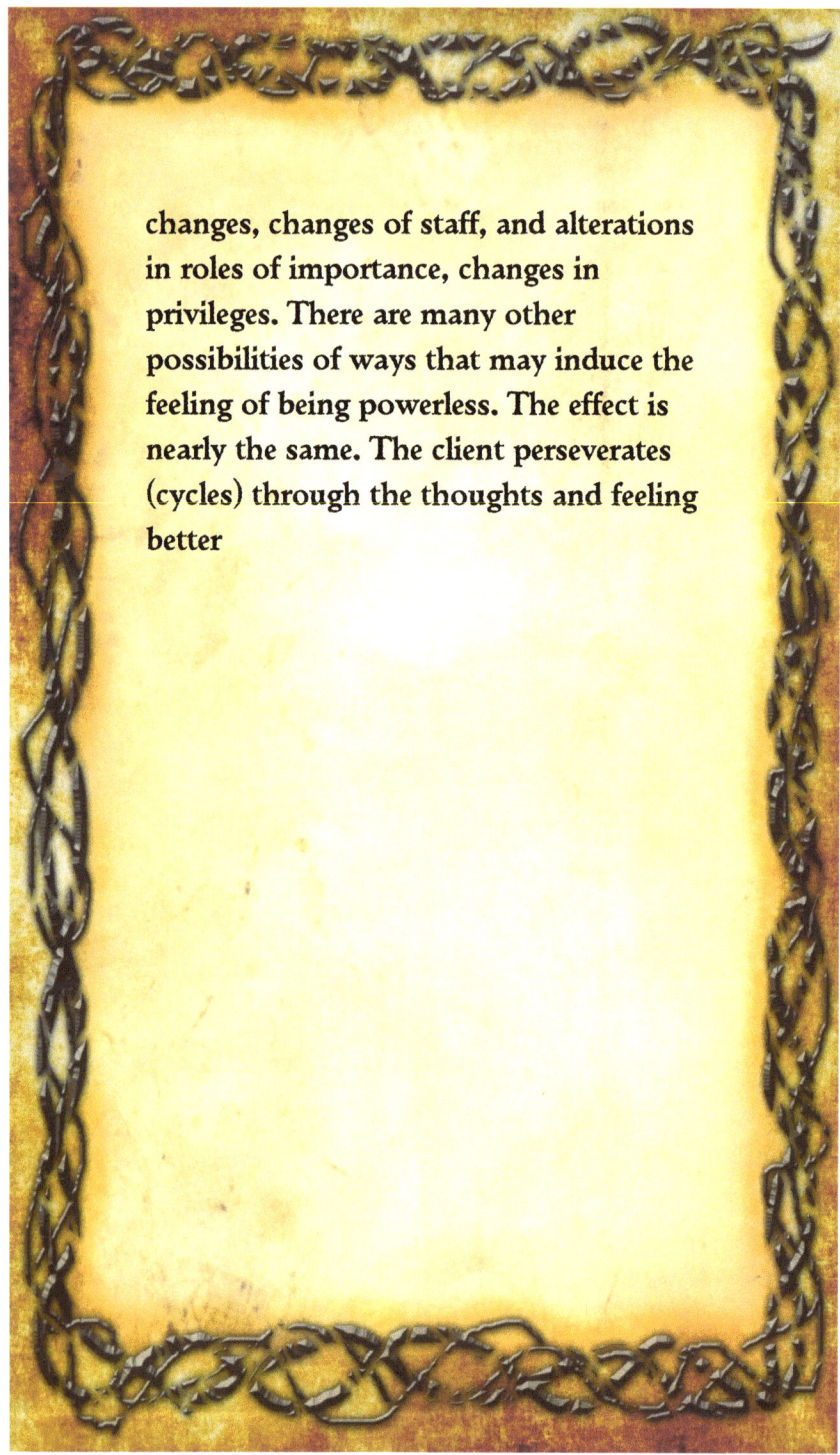

changes, changes of staff, and alterations in roles of importance, changes in privileges. There are many other possibilities of ways that may induce the feeling of being powerless. The effect is nearly the same. The client perseverates (cycles) through the thoughts and feeling better

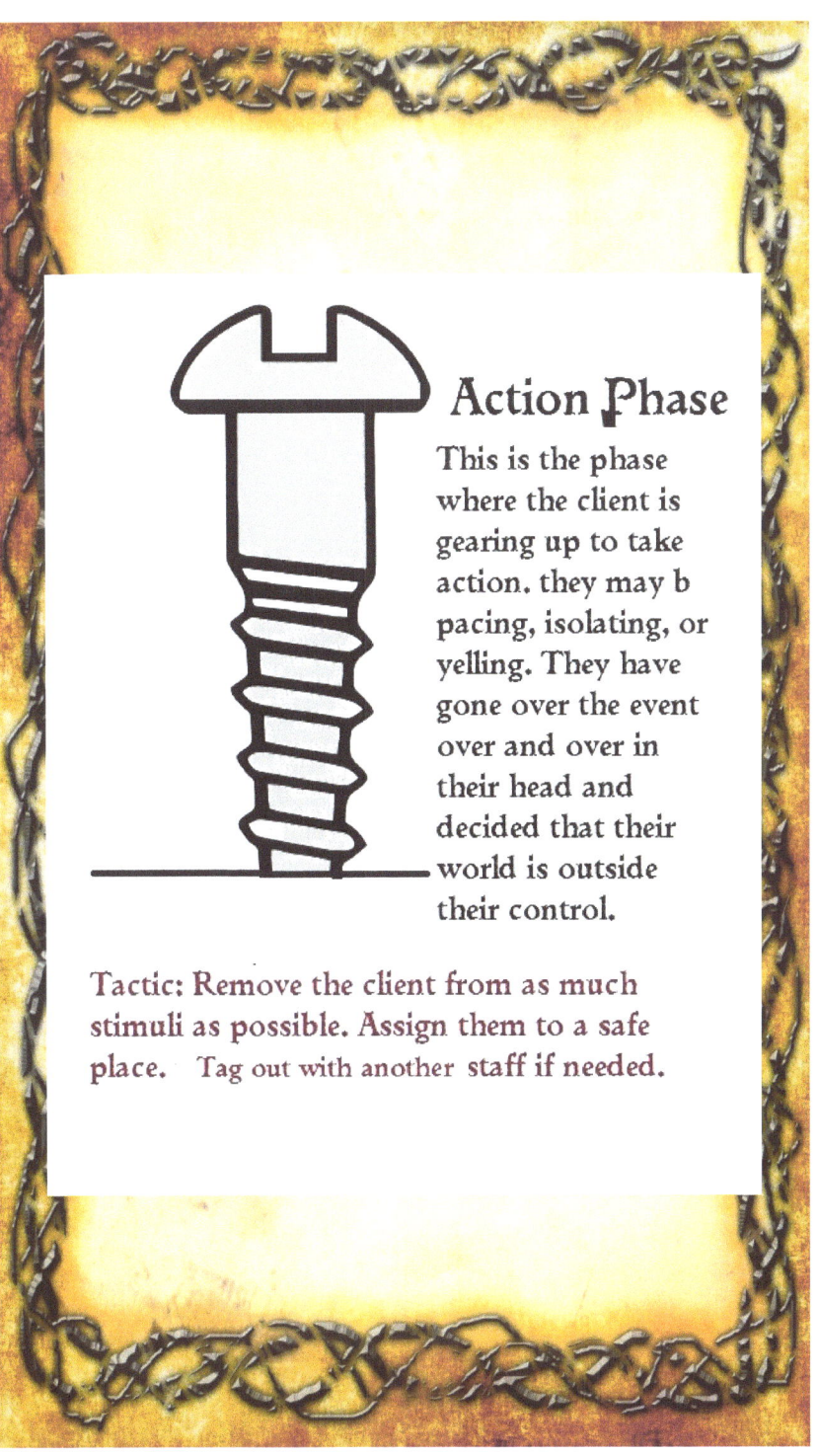

Action Phase

This is the phase where the client is gearing up to take action. they may b pacing, isolating, or yelling. They have gone over the event over and over in their head and decided that their world is outside their control.

Tactic: Remove the client from as much stimuli as possible. Assign them to a safe place.   Tag out with another staff if needed.

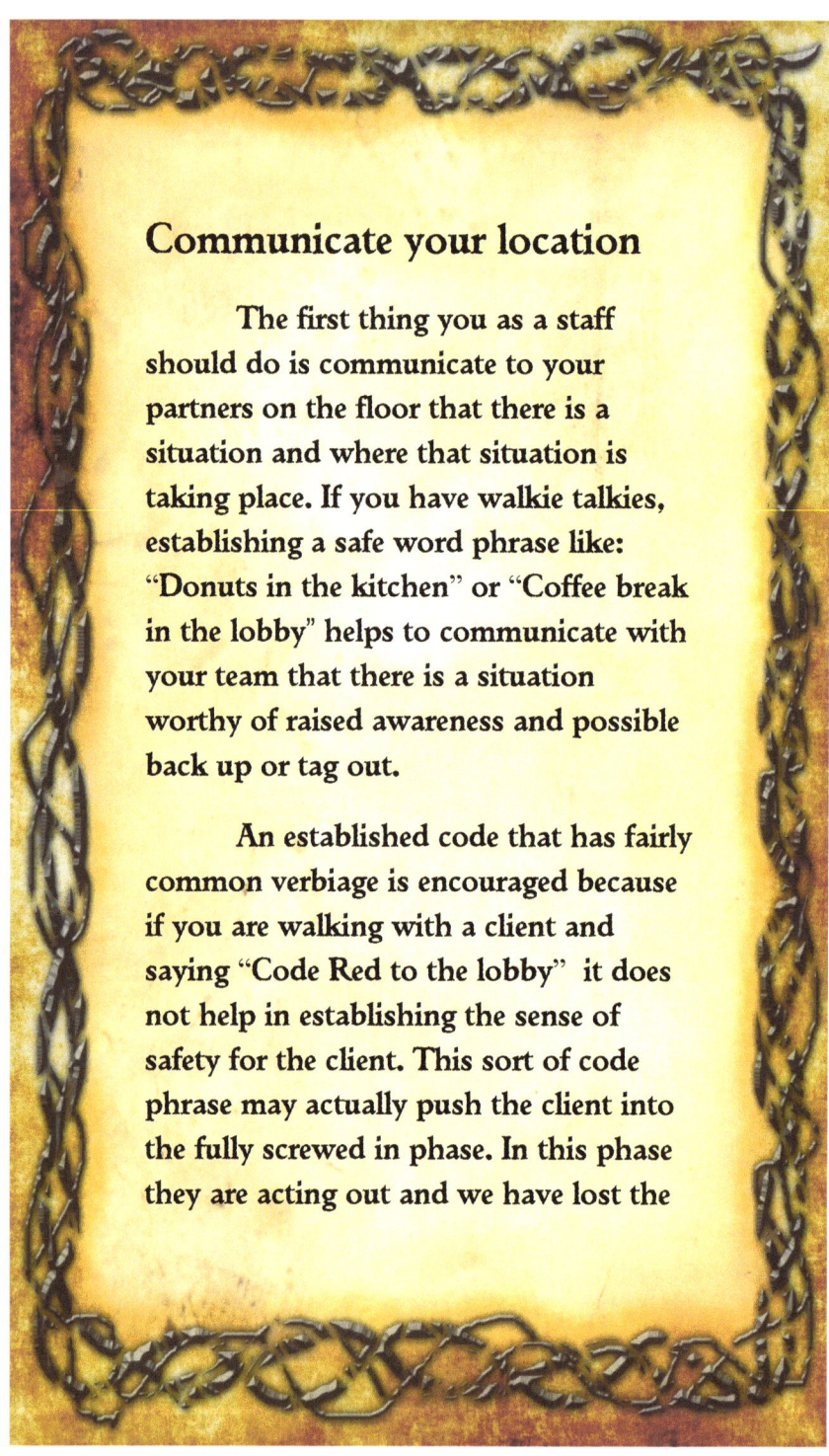

Communicate your location

The first thing you as a staff should do is communicate to your partners on the floor that there is a situation and where that situation is taking place. If you have walkie talkies, establishing a safe word phrase like: "Donuts in the kitchen" or "Coffee break in the lobby" helps to communicate with your team that there is a situation worthy of raised awareness and possible back up or tag out.

An established code that has fairly common verbiage is encouraged because if you are walking with a client and saying "Code Red to the lobby" it does not help in establishing the sense of safety for the client. This sort of code phrase may actually push the client into the fully screwed in phase. In this phase they are acting out and we have lost the

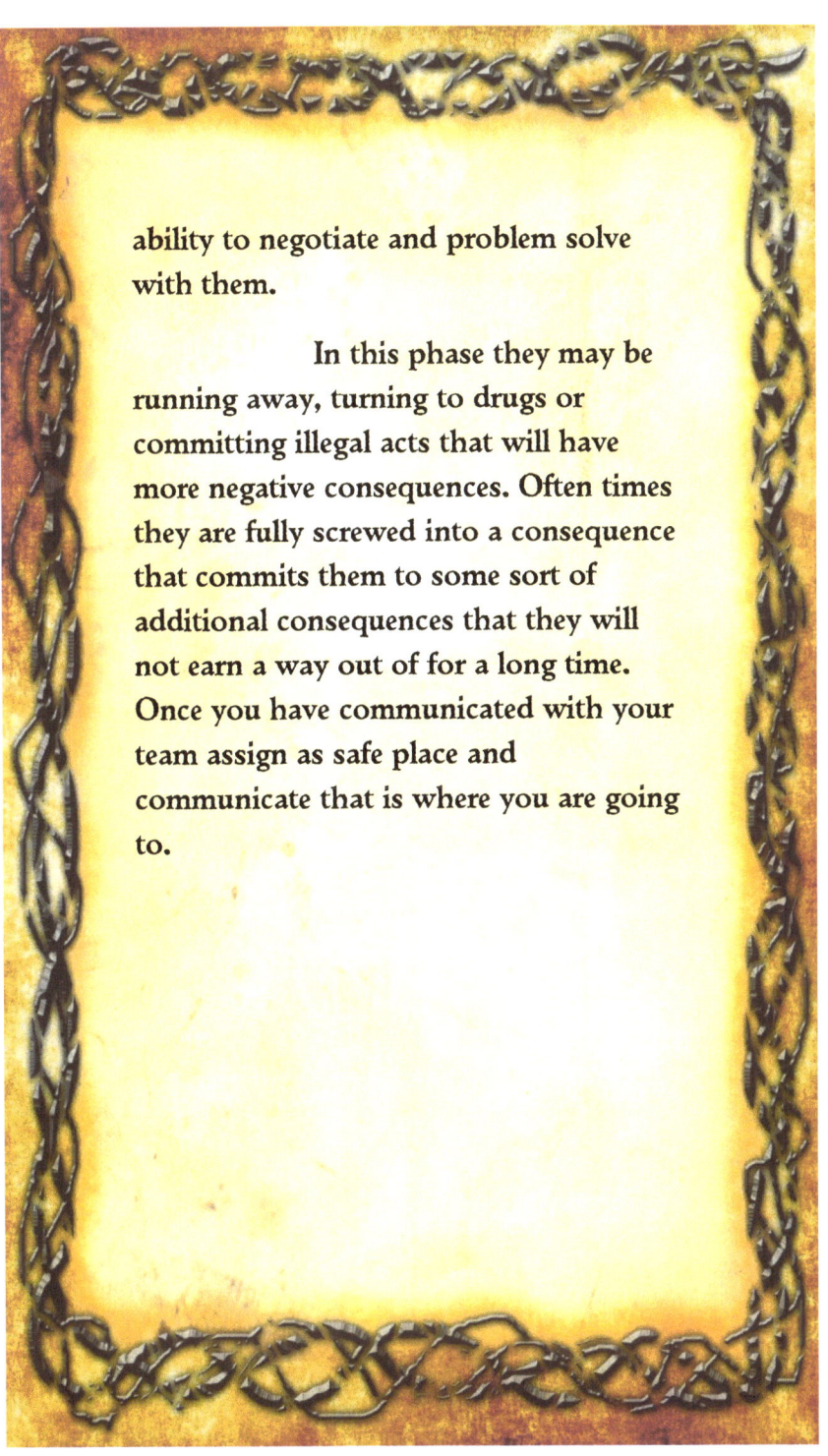

ability to negotiate and problem solve with them.

In this phase they may be running away, turning to drugs or committing illegal acts that will have more negative consequences. Often times they are fully screwed into a consequence that commits them to some sort of additional consequences that they will not earn a way out of for a long time. Once you have communicated with your team assign as safe place and communicate that is where you are going to.

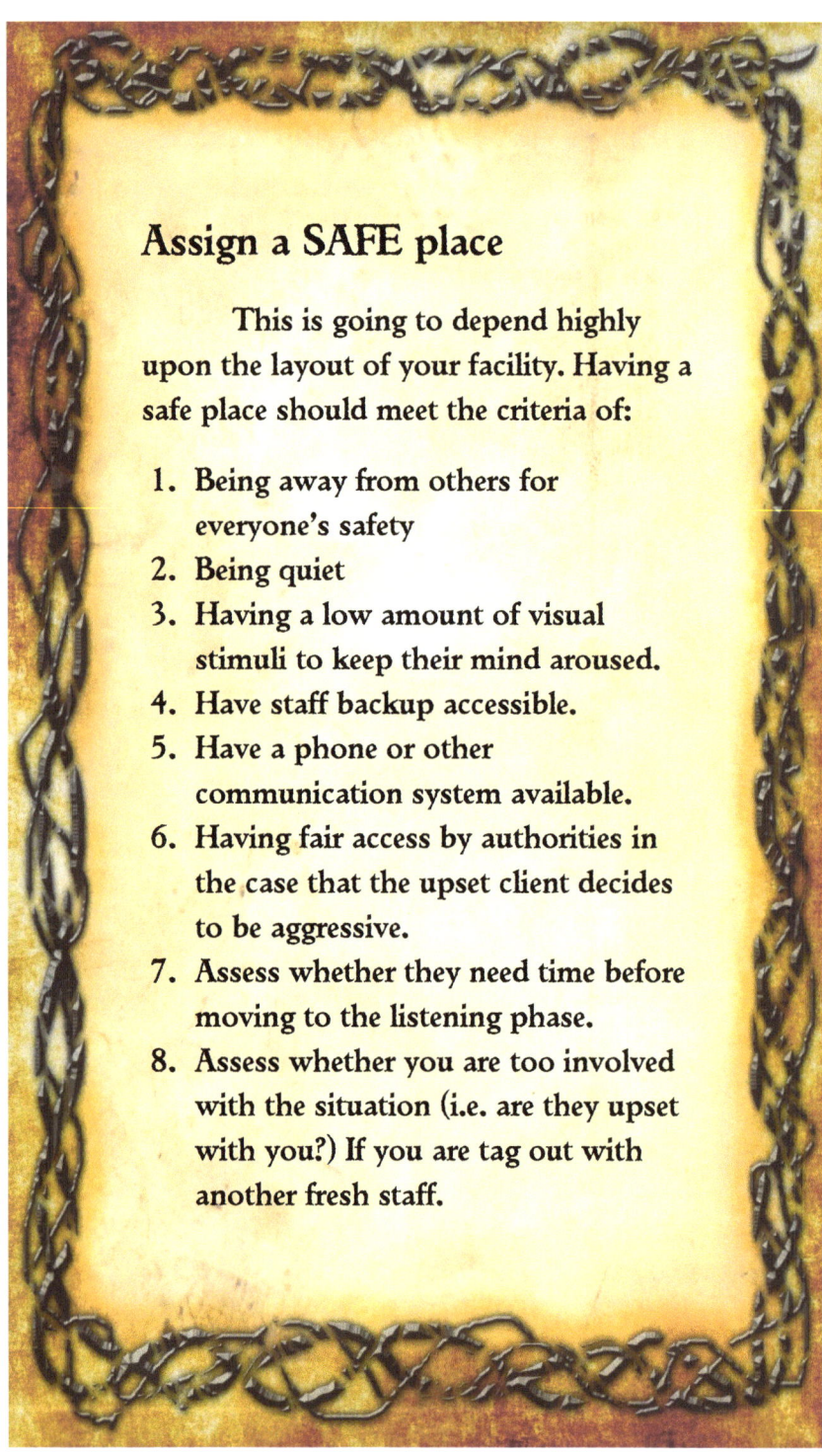

Assign a SAFE place

This is going to depend highly upon the layout of your facility. Having a safe place should meet the criteria of:

1. Being away from others for everyone's safety
2. Being quiet
3. Having a low amount of visual stimuli to keep their mind aroused.
4. Have staff backup accessible.
5. Have a phone or other communication system available.
6. Having fair access by authorities in the case that the upset client decides to be aggressive.
7. Assess whether they need time before moving to the listening phase.
8. Assess whether you are too involved with the situation (i.e. are they upset with you?) If you are tag out with another fresh staff.

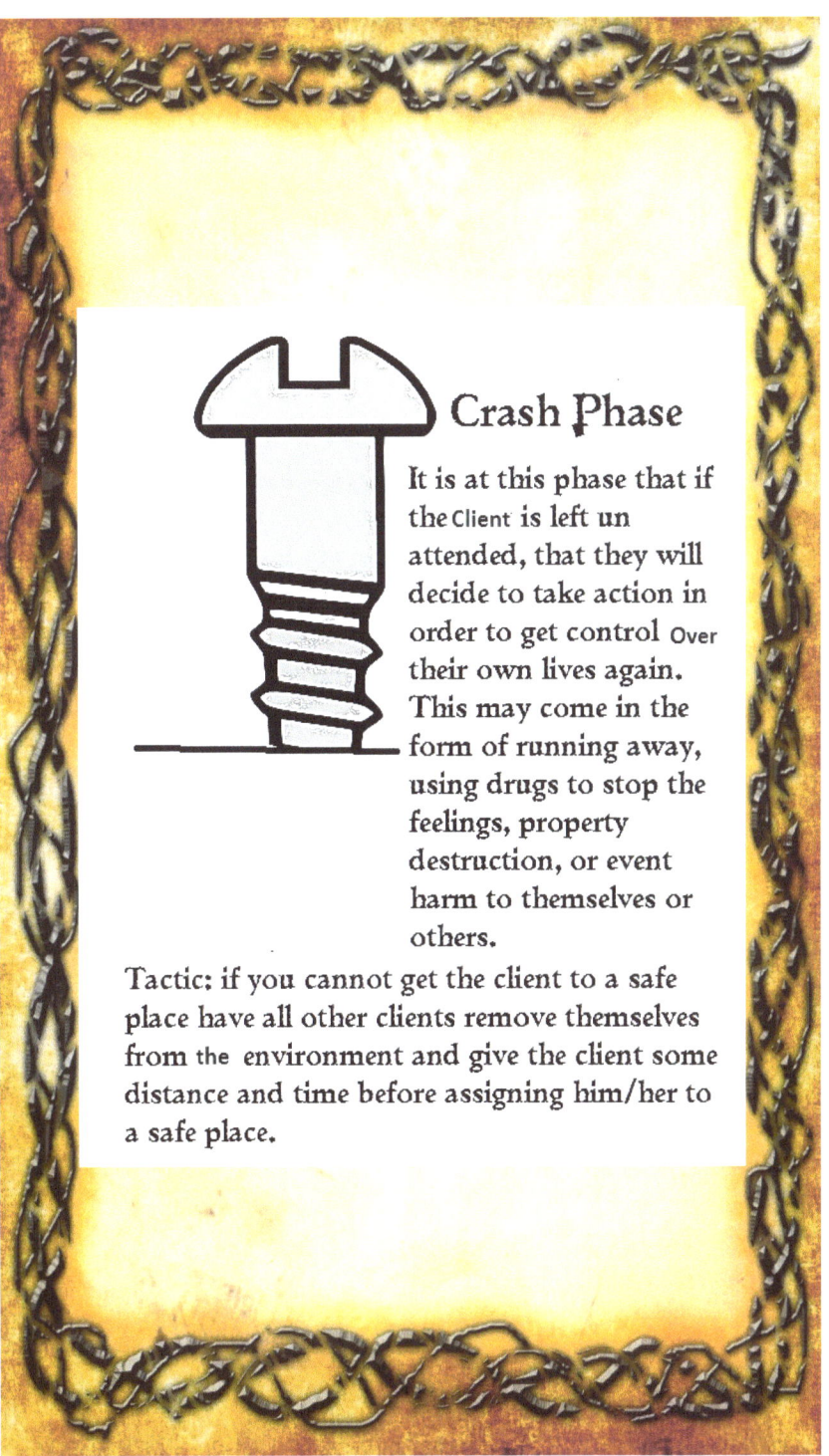

Crash Phase

It is at this phase that if the Client is left un attended, that they will decide to take action in order to get control Over their own lives again. This may come in the form of running away, using drugs to stop the feelings, property destruction, or event harm to themselves or others.

Tactic: if you cannot get the client to a safe place have all other clients remove themselves from the environment and give the client some distance and time before assigning him/her to a safe place.

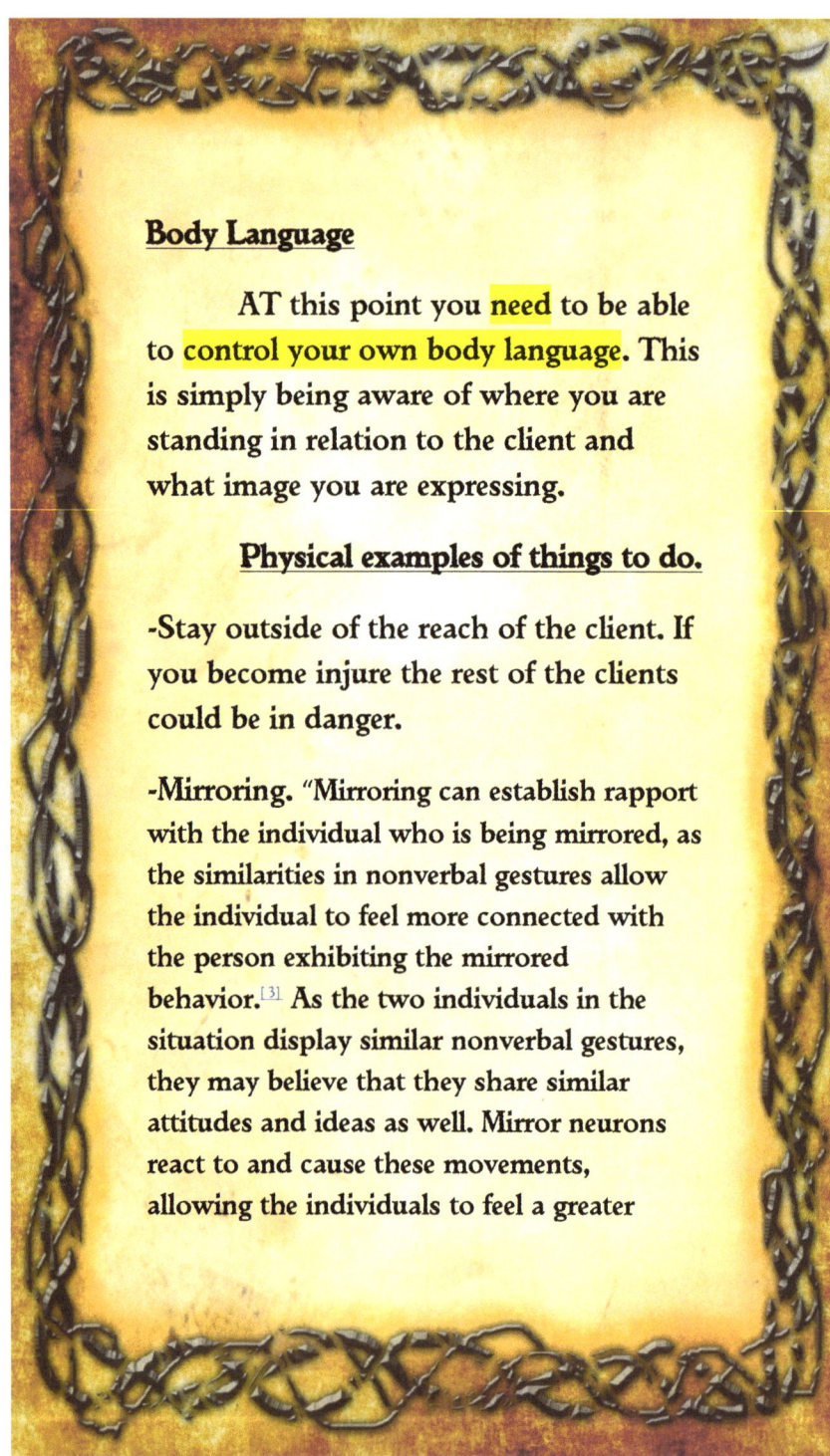

Body Language

AT this point you <mark>need</mark> to be able to <mark>control your own body language</mark>. This is simply being aware of where you are standing in relation to the client and what image you are expressing.

Physical examples of things to do.

-Stay outside of the reach of the client. If you become injure the rest of the clients could be in danger.

-Mirroring. "Mirroring can establish rapport with the individual who is being mirrored, as the similarities in nonverbal gestures allow the individual to feel more connected with the person exhibiting the mirrored behavior.[3] As the two individuals in the situation display similar nonverbal gestures, they may believe that they share similar attitudes and ideas as well. Mirror neurons react to and cause these movements, allowing the individuals to feel a greater sense of engagement and belonging within the situation." (Wikipedia 2016)

- Keep your hands open and relaxed.

- Lean in and portray listening intently.

Do not

1. Do not square off, or square your shoulders with the client.
2. Do not make them uncomfortable by standing over them.
3. Nod up and down in agreement when necessary.

Active Listening

This skill can be done at any phase. The best sort of listening is active listening because that means that the client who is venting has the opportunity to feel that they are being cared for. There is no time limit on caring.

"Active listening is a communication technique used in counseling, training, and conflict resolution. It requires that the listener fully concentrates, understands, responds and then remembers what is being said.[1] This is opposed to reflective listening where the listener repeats back to the speaker what they have just heard to confirm understanding of both parties".^(Wikipedia 2016)

1. Comprehending (Let them Vent)

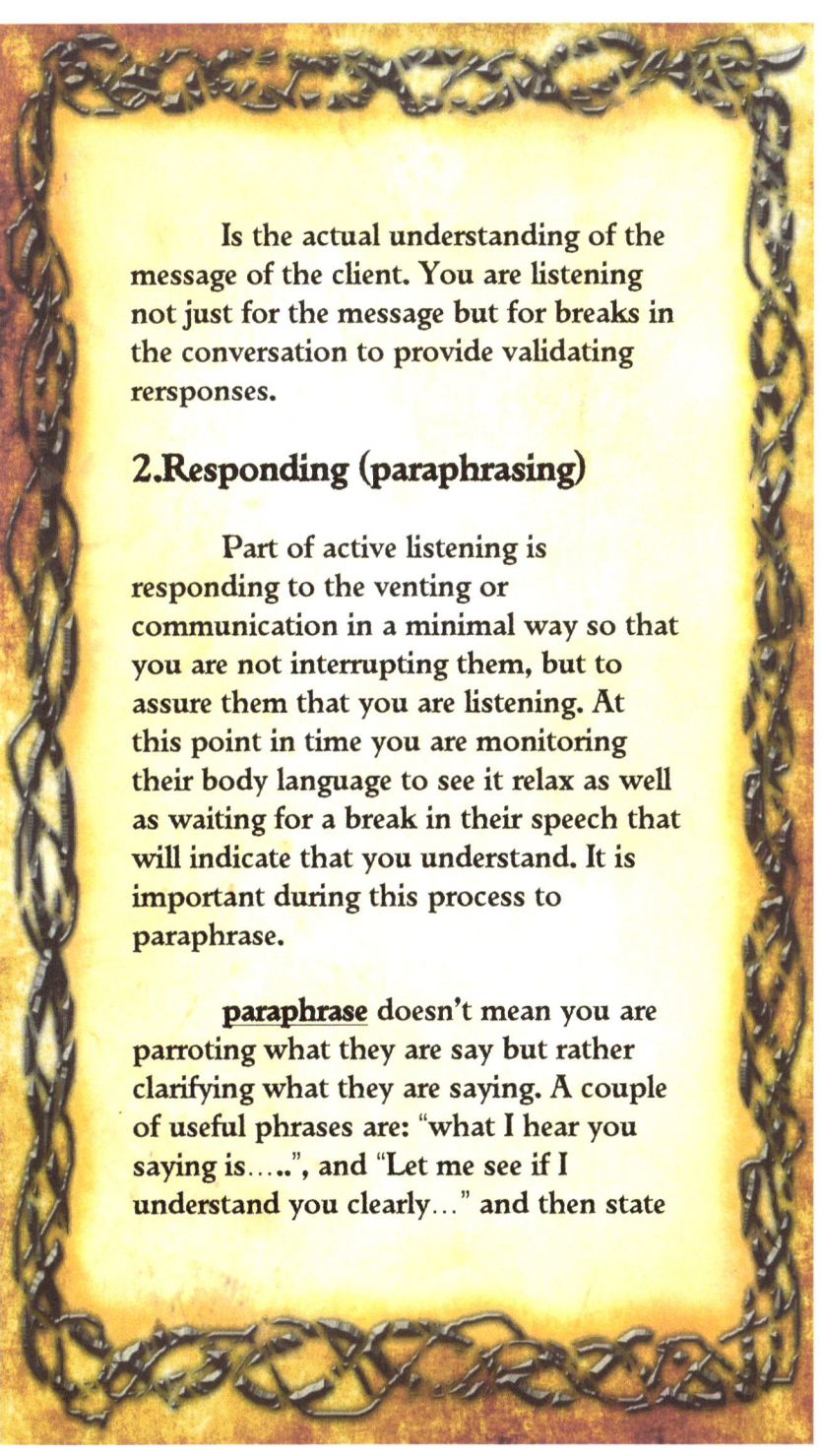

Is the actual understanding of the message of the client. You are listening not just for the message but for breaks in the conversation to provide validating rersponses.

2.Responding (paraphrasing)

Part of active listening is responding to the venting or communication in a minimal way so that you are not interrupting them, but to assure them that you are listening. At this point in time you are monitoring their body language to see it relax as well as waiting for a break in their speech that will indicate that you understand. It is important during this process to paraphrase.

paraphrase doesn't mean you are parroting what they are say but rather clarifying what they are saying. A couple of useful phrases are: "what I hear you saying is…..", and "Let me see if I understand you clearly…" and then state

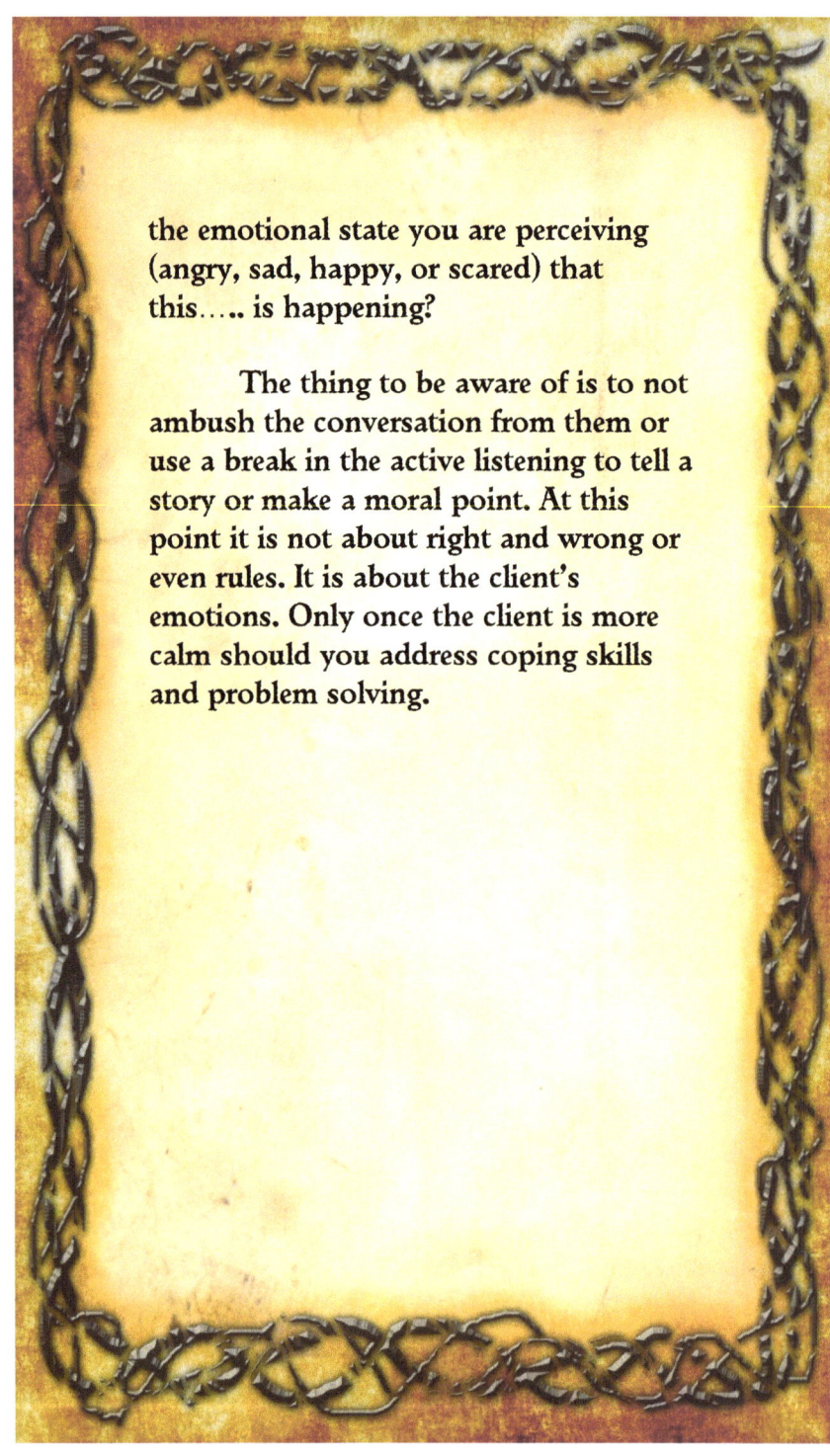

the emotional state you are perceiving (angry, sad, happy, or scared) that this….. is happening?

The thing to be aware of is to not ambush the conversation from them or use a break in the active listening to tell a story or make a moral point. At this point it is not about right and wrong or even rules. It is about the client's emotions. Only once the client is more calm should you address coping skills and problem solving.

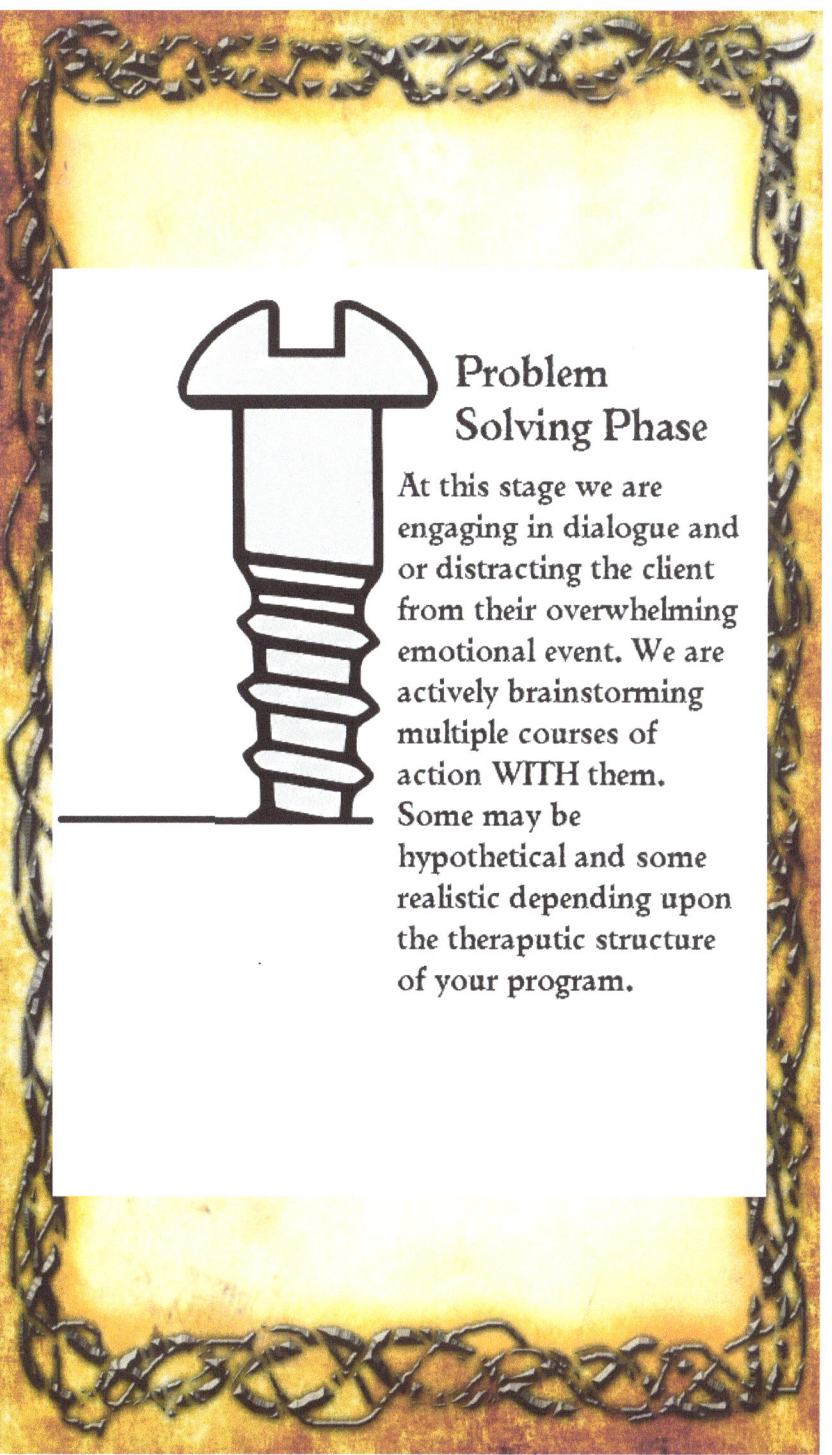

Problem Solving Phase

At this stage we are engaging in dialogue and or distracting the client from their overwhelming emotional event. We are actively brainstorming multiple courses of action WITH them. Some may be hypothetical and some realistic depending upon the theraputic structure of your program.

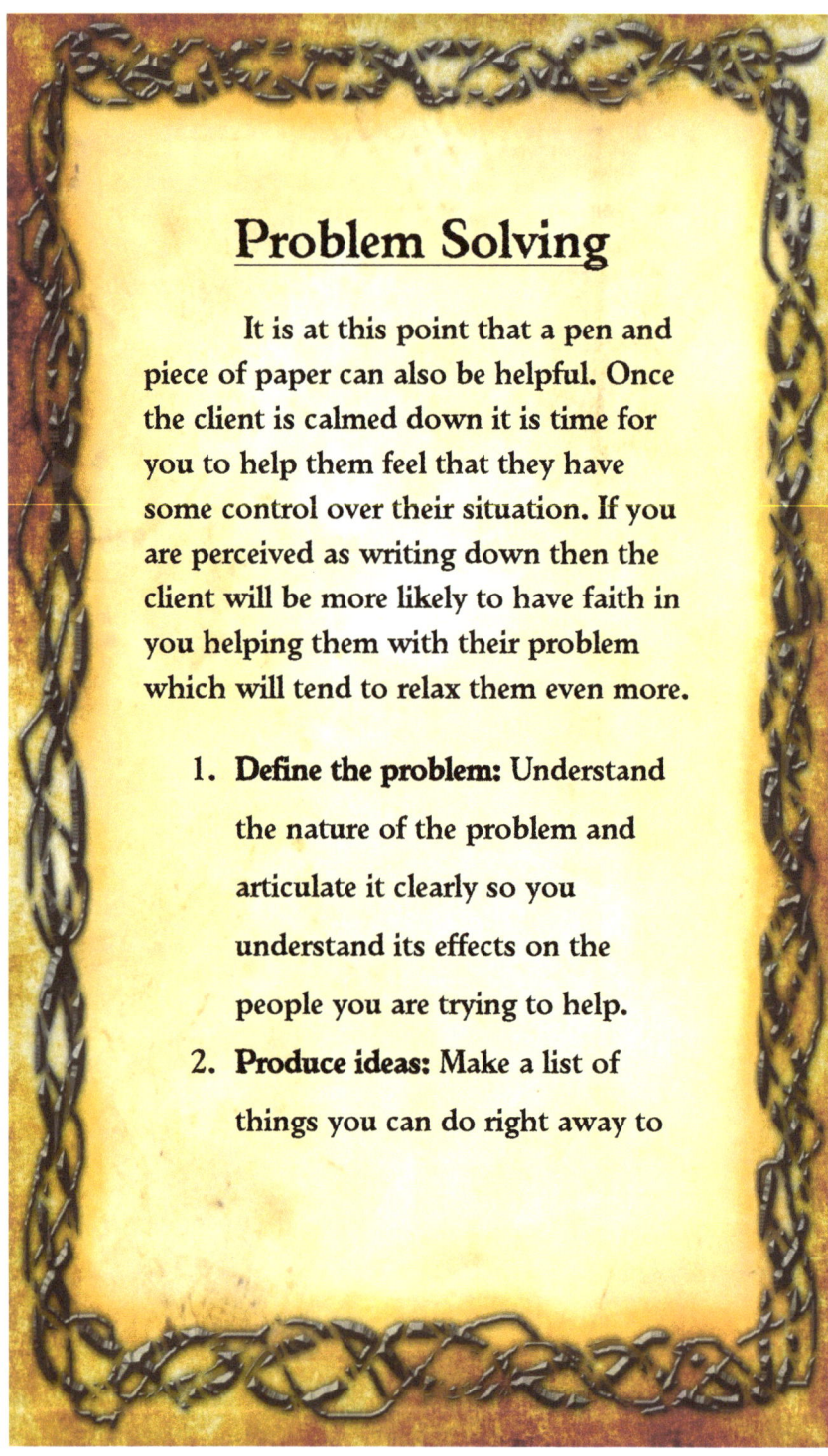

Problem Solving

It is at this point that a pen and piece of paper can also be helpful. Once the client is calmed down it is time for you to help them feel that they have some control over their situation. If you are perceived as writing down then the client will be more likely to have faith in you helping them with their problem which will tend to relax them even more.

1. **Define the problem:** Understand the nature of the problem and articulate it clearly so you understand its effects on the people you are trying to help.

2. **Produce ideas:** Make a list of things you can do right away to

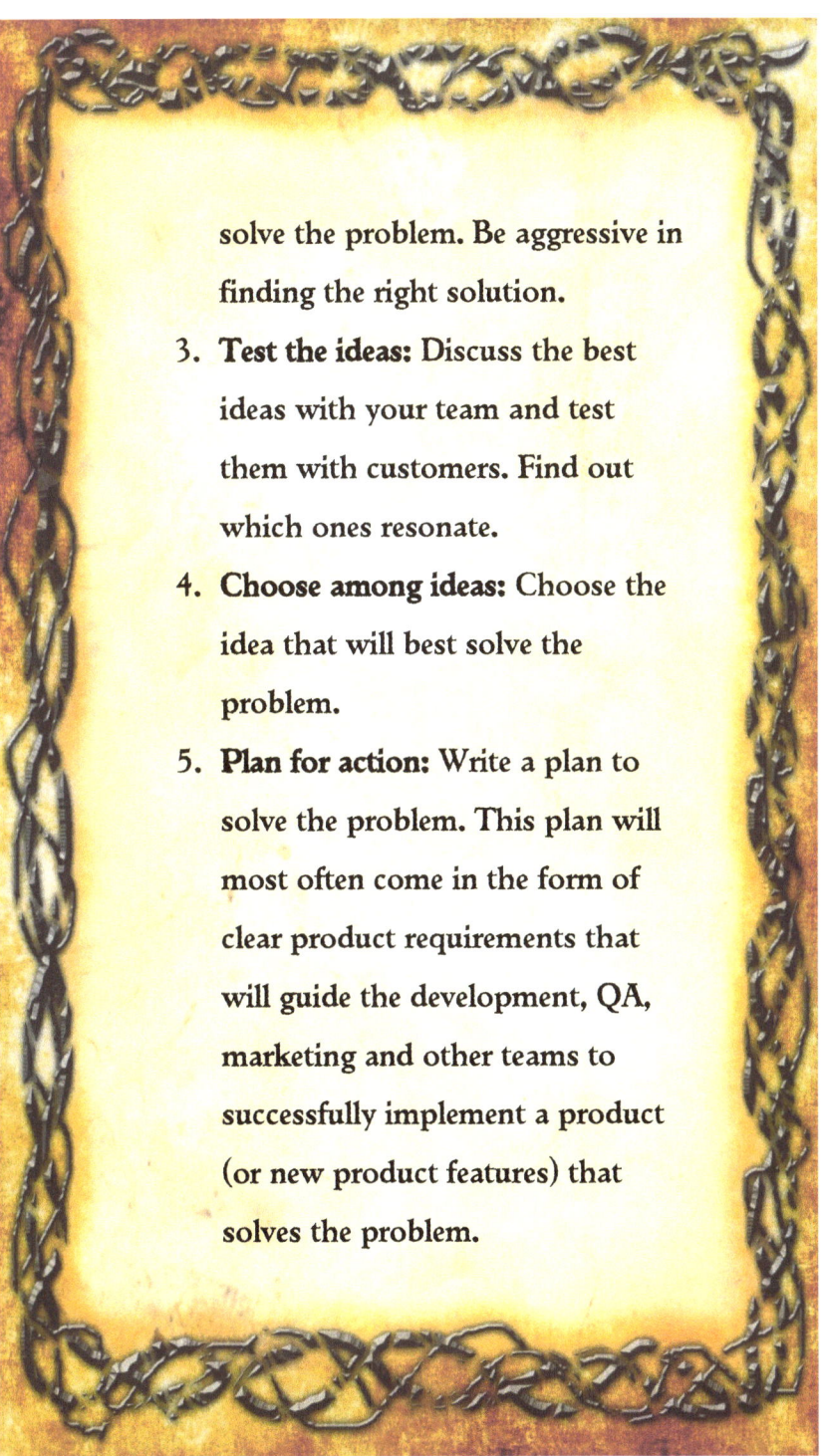

solve the problem. Be aggressive in finding the right solution.

3. **Test the ideas:** Discuss the best ideas with your team and test them with customers. Find out which ones resonate.

4. **Choose among ideas:** Choose the idea that will best solve the problem.

5. **Plan for action:** Write a plan to solve the problem. This plan will most often come in the form of clear product requirements that will guide the development, QA, marketing and other teams to successfully implement a product (or new product features) that solves the problem.

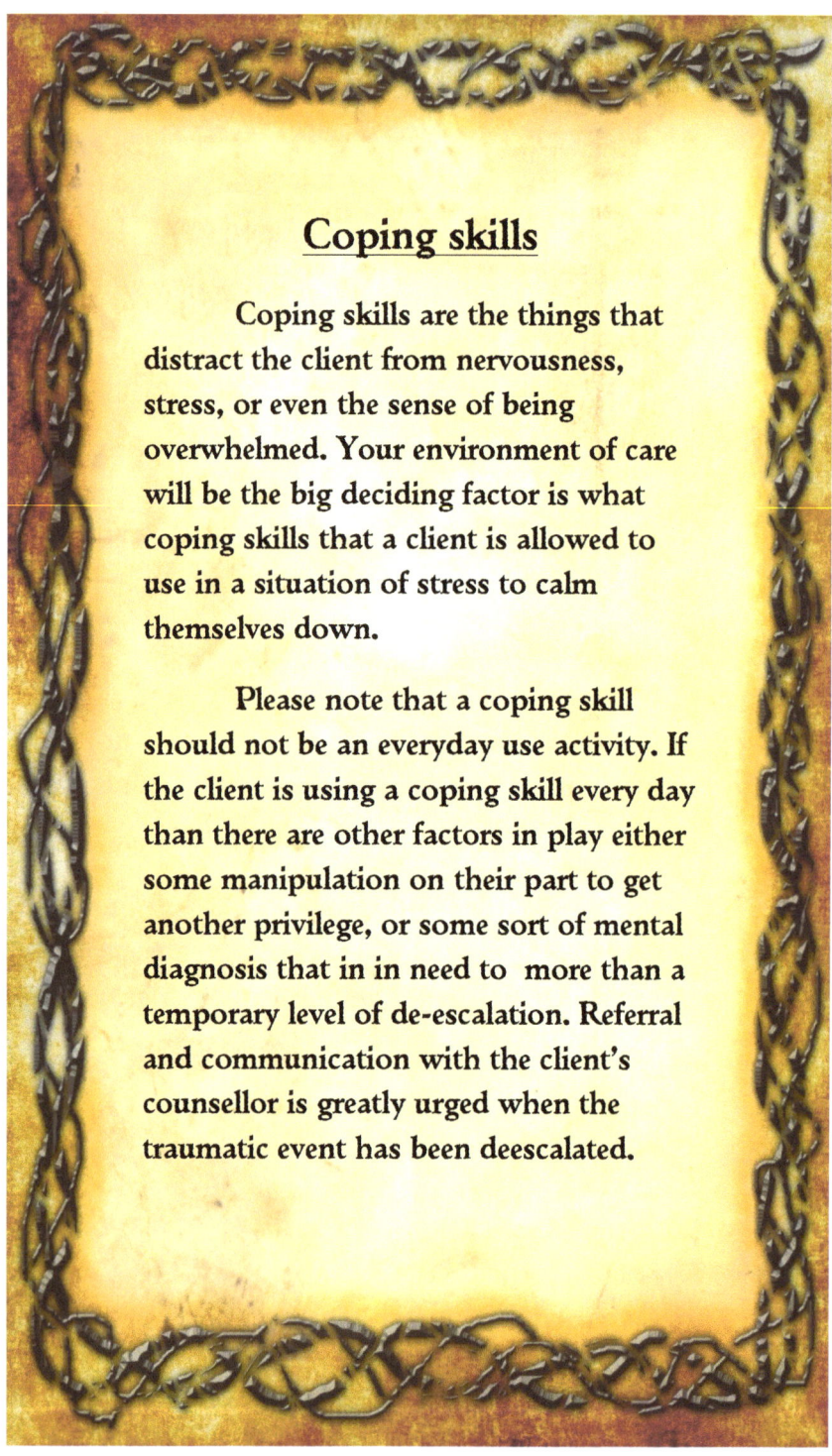

Coping skills

Coping skills are the things that distract the client from nervousness, stress, or even the sense of being overwhelmed. Your environment of care will be the big deciding factor is what coping skills that a client is allowed to use in a situation of stress to calm themselves down.

Please note that a coping skill should not be an everyday use activity. If the client is using a coping skill every day than there are other factors in play either some manipulation on their part to get another privilege, or some sort of mental diagnosis that in in need to more than a temporary level of de-escalation. Referral and communication with the client's counsellor is greatly urged when the traumatic event has been deescalated.

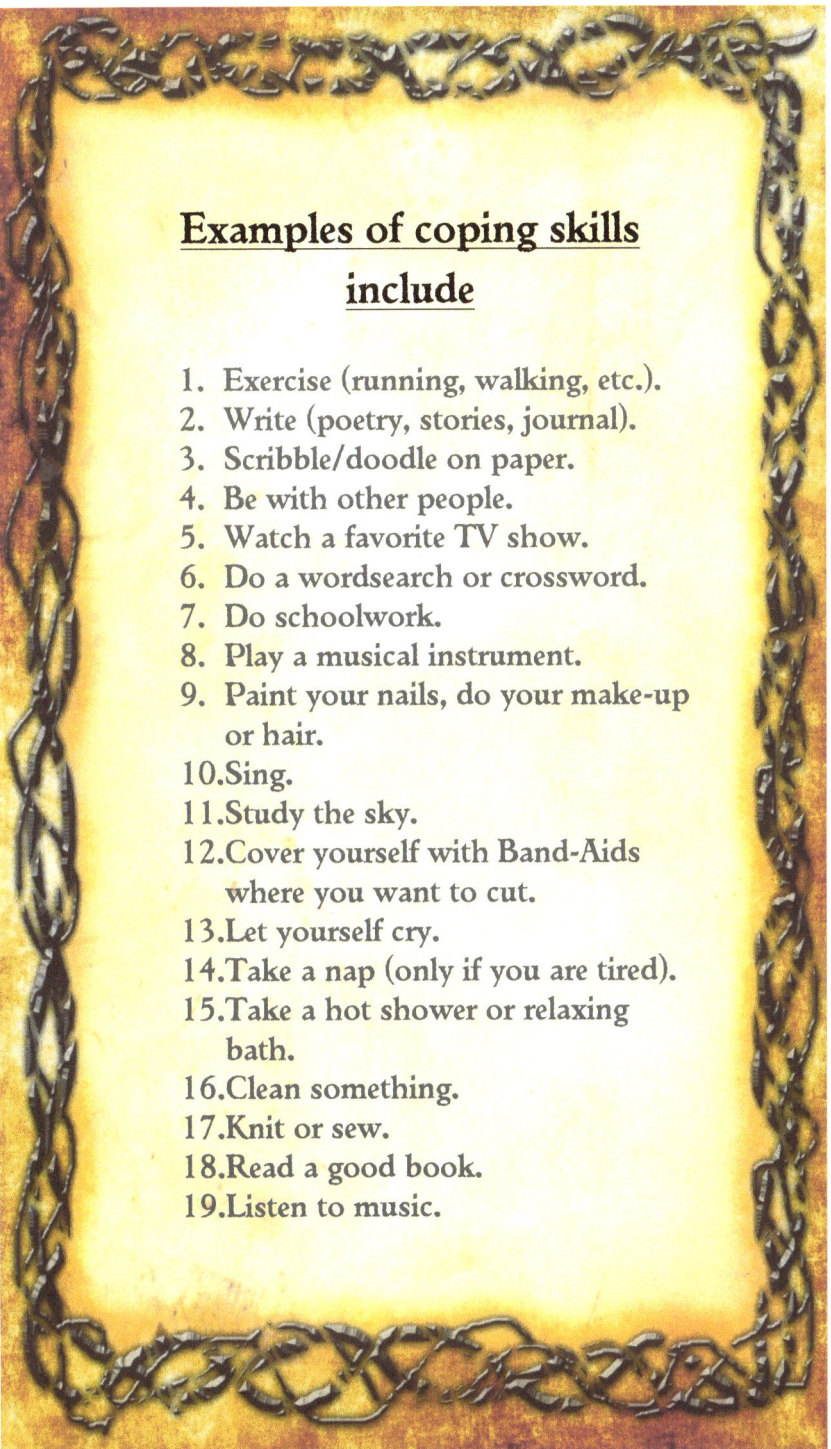

Examples of coping skills include

1. Exercise (running, walking, etc.).
2. Write (poetry, stories, journal).
3. Scribble/doodle on paper.
4. Be with other people.
5. Watch a favorite TV show.
6. Do a wordsearch or crossword.
7. Do schoolwork.
8. Play a musical instrument.
9. Paint your nails, do your make-up or hair.
10. Sing.
11. Study the sky.
12. Cover yourself with Band-Aids where you want to cut.
13. Let yourself cry.
14. Take a nap (only if you are tired).
15. Take a hot shower or relaxing bath.
16. Clean something.
17. Knit or sew.
18. Read a good book.
19. Listen to music.

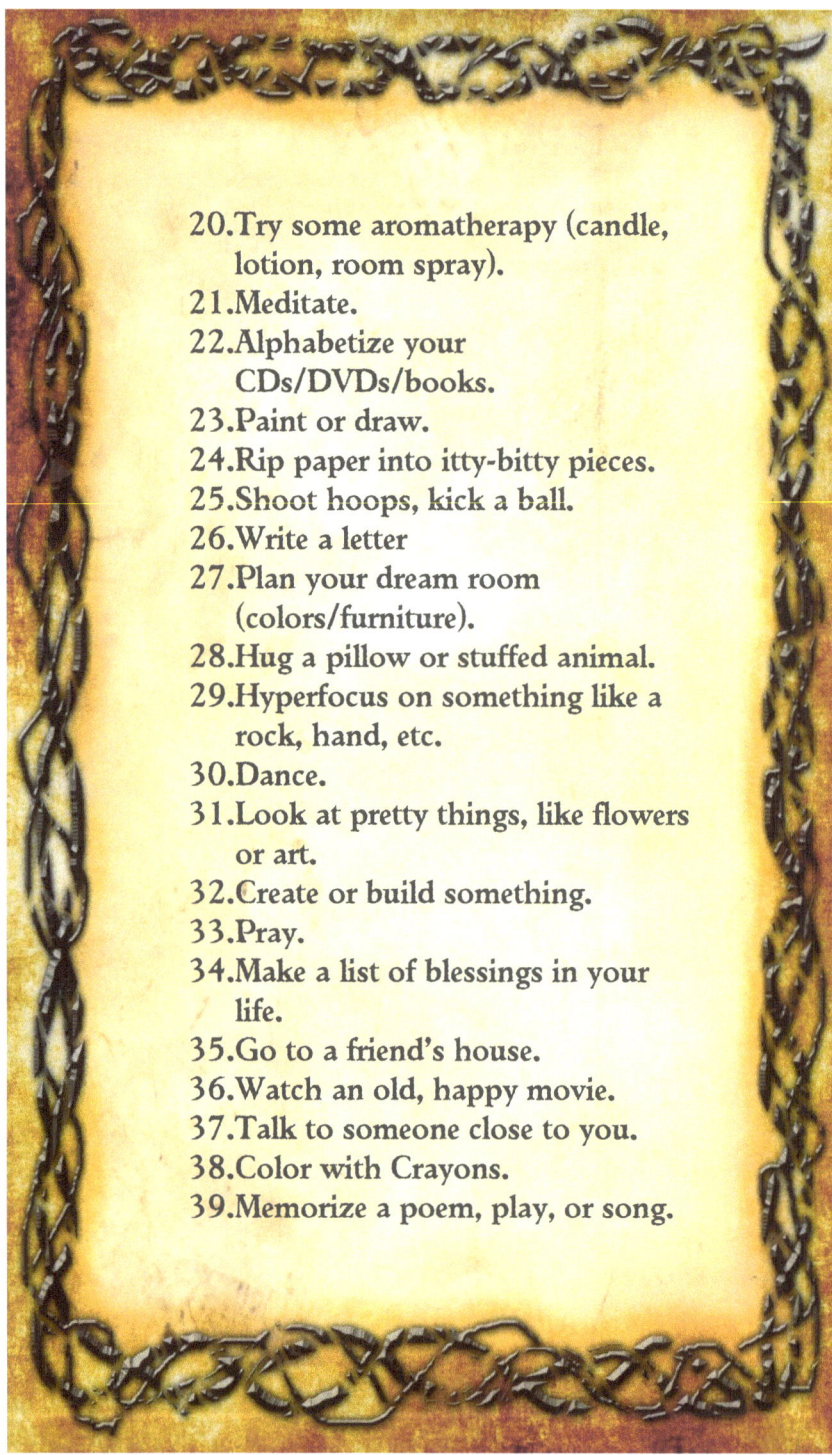

20. Try some aromatherapy (candle, lotion, room spray).
21. Meditate.
22. Alphabetize your CDs/DVDs/books.
23. Paint or draw.
24. Rip paper into itty-bitty pieces.
25. Shoot hoops, kick a ball.
26. Write a letter
27. Plan your dream room (colors/furniture).
28. Hug a pillow or stuffed animal.
29. Hyperfocus on something like a rock, hand, etc.
30. Dance.
31. Look at pretty things, like flowers or art.
32. Create or build something.
33. Pray.
34. Make a list of blessings in your life.
35. Go to a friend's house.
36. Watch an old, happy movie.
37. Talk to someone close to you.
38. Color with Crayons.
39. Memorize a poem, play, or song.

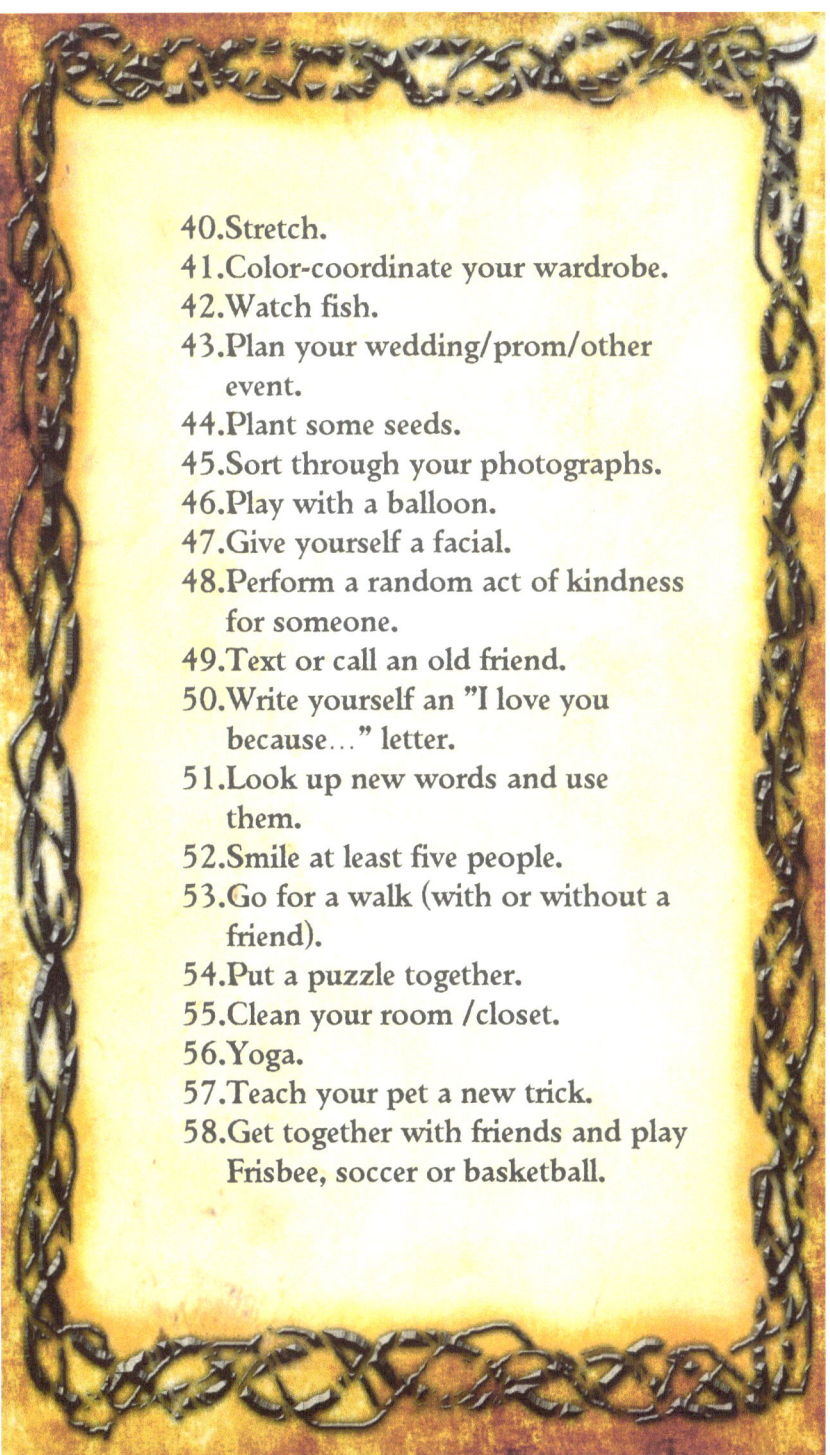

40. Stretch.
41. Color-coordinate your wardrobe.
42. Watch fish.
43. Plan your wedding/prom/other event.
44. Plant some seeds.
45. Sort through your photographs.
46. Play with a balloon.
47. Give yourself a facial.
48. Perform a random act of kindness for someone.
49. Text or call an old friend.
50. Write yourself an "I love you because…" letter.
51. Look up new words and use them.
52. Smile at least five people.
53. Go for a walk (with or without a friend).
54. Put a puzzle together.
55. Clean your room /closet.
56. Yoga.
57. Teach your pet a new trick.
58. Get together with friends and play Frisbee, soccer or basketball.

59.Make a list of goals for the
week/month/year/5 years.

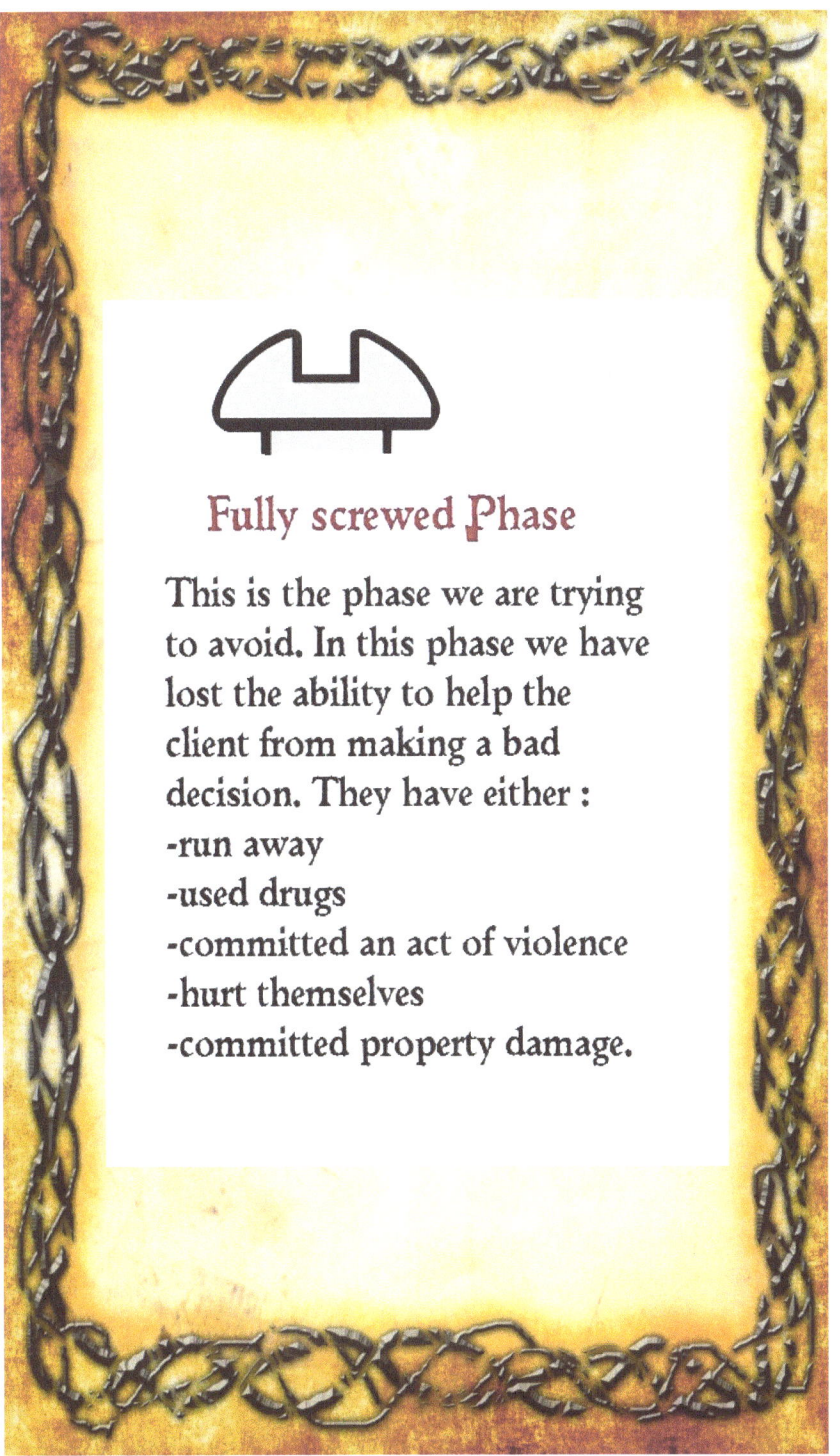

Fully screwed Phase

This is the phase we are trying to avoid. In this phase we have lost the ability to help the client from making a bad decision. They have either :
-run away
-used drugs
-committed an act of violence
-hurt themselves
-committed property damage.

Quiz

1. List the phases 5 of Traumatic Event Management?

2. What are 3 examples of possible abnormal body language.

3. What are the 4 most common emotions that can be overwhelming?

4. What are 2 of the outside influences that can create a traumatic event for the client?

5. What are two inside the facility, influences that can create a traumatic event for the client?

6. List 2 things that you should have when assigning a safe place?

7. What are the two main parts of active listening?

8. What needs to happen before we problem solve.

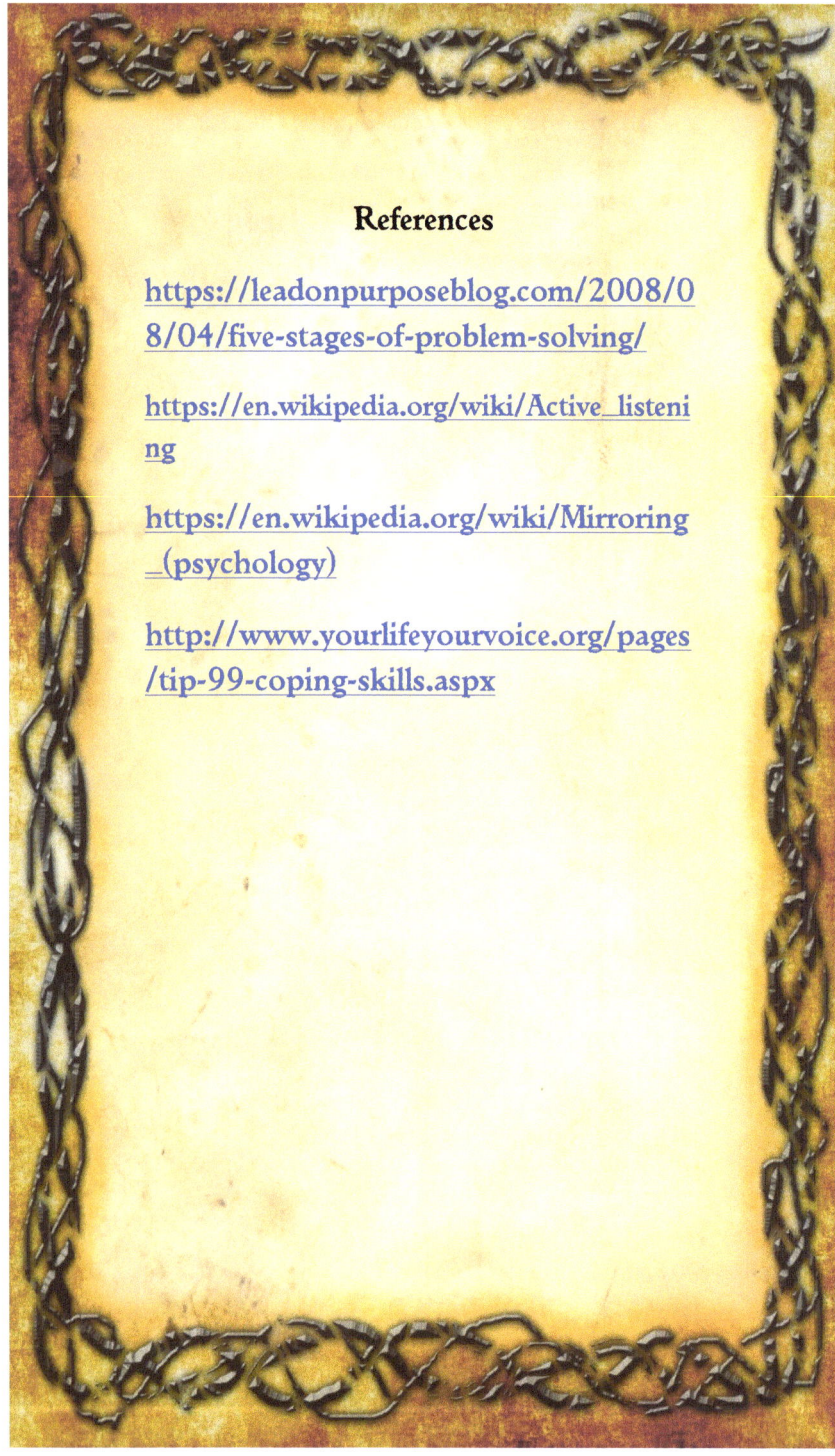

References

https://leadonpurposeblog.com/2008/08/04/five-stages-of-problem-solving/

https://en.wikipedia.org/wiki/Active_listening

https://en.wikipedia.org/wiki/Mirroring_(psychology)

http://www.yourlifeyourvoice.org/pages/tip-99-coping-skills.aspx

Roger Huntman A.A., B.S. and M.Ed, has worked in the fields of mental health, chemical addiction, and law enforcement since 1997. He currently works in the field and occasionally does speaking engagements on mental health and addiction.